35 Is Not the Age to Go Quiet

Ebony Greenfield, M.Ed

35 Is Not the Age to Go Quiet

Follow & Connect

Facebook: **ImJarra**
Instagram: **@ImJarra**
YouTube: **ImJarra**

© **Ebony Greenfield**
All rights reserved.

No part of this book may be reproduced, distributed, or transmitted in any form or by any means without written permission from the author, except for brief quotations in reviews.

This book is intended for personal reflection and spiritual growth. The content is not a substitute for professional medical, psychological, or pastoral counseling.

About This Book

This book was designed to be interactive and personal.
Write freely. Reflect honestly. Move at your own pace.

You may view and edit this book across supported devices, including Mac, iPad, and iPhone. Feel free to personalize fonts, styles, and spacing as you make this book your own.

Author

Ebony Greenfield, M.Ed

Dedication

This book is for the version of me that survived everything —
and for the version of you who did too.

All glory to **God**, for His grace, patience, and faithfulness.
To my **mama**, thank you for your love and strength.
In loving memory of **Mike** — rest in heaven.

And to **you**, the reader —
thank you for choosing to stay, reflect, and grow.
May these pages remind you that your life still matters, and your voice is not done yet.

Your Reflection

Count how many **True** answers you selected.

If you answered True to 7–10 statements

You are not broken — you are tired, honest, and ready.
This book is meant to help you reconnect with yourself and with God in a gentle, steady way. Move slowly through the pages. Let God meet you where you are, not where you think you should be.

If you answered True to 4–6 statements

You are at a crossroads. Some parts of your life feel stable, while others feel quietly unsettled. This book will help you listen more closely, name what's been buried, and decide what you're ready to grow again.

If you answered True to 0–3 statements

You may feel grounded right now, but that doesn't mean there's nothing here for you. This book can help deepen what's already working, strengthen your spiritual rhythm, and protect the life you're building from shrinking over time.

Final Invitation

However you answered, there is nothing to fix — only something to notice.
This book isn't here to rush you. It's here to walk with you.

When you're ready, turn the page.

1

Do Not Shrink Your Life

Scripture
"Do not despise these small beginnings, for the Lord rejoices to see the work begin."
— Zechariah 4:10

Biblical Reflection

Has the Lord ever asked you to start small, even when you knew what He showed you would one day be greater? He did the same with His people. When Israel returned from exile, God asked them to rebuild the temple — not as it once was, but as it could be again. What stood before them felt unimpressive and unfinished, and some of them wept at how small the beginning looked.

The Lord spoke to remind them that He was not disappointed by the foundation. He rejoiced in it. God does not wait for things to look complete before He calls them good. Often, He begins quietly so we learn to trust Him before we see the fullness of what He promised. If your life feels smaller than you imagined right now, it does not mean God has changed His mind. It may simply mean He is building again.

Invitation to Stillness

Take a moment to sit quietly with this scripture.
Breathe slowly.
Let the words settle without trying to fix or analyze anything.
Simply notice what rises in you.

Writing Prompt

Set a timer for **10 minutes**.
As you listen to your favorite uplifting or worship song, write about one area of your life where you have been shrinking — emotionally, spiritually, creatively, or mentally.

Ask yourself gently:

Where did I start playing smaller than I truly am?

What part of me have I been minimizing to feel safe?

Write honestly. This is between you and God.

Inner Goal / Mindset Shift

Today, I release the belief that I must shrink to survive.
I allow myself to take up the space God designed for me.
I trust that what He began in me is still worthy of care, faith, and attention.

2. God Is Not Intimidated by Time

Scripture
"So now, go. I am sending you to Pharaoh to bring my people the Israelites out of Egypt."
— **Exodus 3:10**

Biblical Reflection

Has God ever spoken purpose over your life at a time that felt inconvenient or late? He did this with Moses. Moses was eighty years old when God called him from the burning bush. He had already lived several lives — prince, fugitive, shepherd — and likely believed his chance to matter had passed.

Yet God was not concerned with Moses' age, pace, or past. God spoke to him as if the calling had been waiting patiently for the right moment. What Moses saw as delay, God saw as preparation. Time had not weakened God's plan — it had strengthened it.

Invitation to Stillness

Take a moment to sit quietly with this scripture.
Breathe slowly.
Let the idea of God's timing settle into your body.
Notice any resistance or relief that rises.

Writing Prompt

Set a timer for **10 minutes**.
As you write, imagine God speaking to you without urgency or disappointment.

Ask yourself gently:

Where have I assumed it is too late for God to use me?

What parts of my past might God be using as preparation instead of punishment?

Write honestly. This is between you and God.

Inner Goal / Mindset Shift

Today, I release the belief that time works against me.
I trust that God's calling is not weakened by age, delay, or detours.
I remain open to what He is still unfolding in my life.

3. You Are Still Being Called

Scripture
"Before I formed you in the womb I knew you, before you were born I set you apart."
— Jeremiah 1:5

Biblical Reflection

Jeremiah believed he was too young and unqualified when God called him. He tried to excuse himself, explaining why he wasn't ready. But God did not agree with Jeremiah's assessment of his life. God reminded him that the calling existed before the fear ever showed up.

God does not wait for confidence to appear before He speaks purpose. His calling is not canceled by doubt, age, or hesitation. If you still feel a pull toward something meaningful, it may be because God is still calling.

Invitation to Stillness

Sit quietly with this scripture.
Breathe in slowly.
Allow yourself to consider that God may still be speaking.
Notice what stirs in your heart.

Writing Prompt

Set a timer for **10 minutes**.

What calling or desire have I been trying to ignore or quiet?

What fear comes up when I imagine saying yes to it?

Write honestly. This is between you and God.

Inner Goal / Mindset Shift

Today, I accept that God's calling still applies to me.
I stop dismissing what He continues to place on my heart.

4. Small Does Not Mean Insignificant

Scripture
"Whoever is faithful with little will also be faithful with much."
— Luke 16:10

Biblical Reflection

David was not chosen because he looked ready. He was chosen while tending sheep, unseen and overlooked. What appeared small to others was where God was shaping his heart. David's obedience in private mattered just as much as his victory in public.

God often starts with what feels small so we learn faithfulness before responsibility. The size of the assignment has never determined its importance.

Invitation to Stillness

Pause and breathe.
Let go of comparison.
Ask God to show you the value of what you are already carrying.

Writing Prompt

Set a timer for **10 minutes**.

What small responsibility or gift have I been undervaluing?

How might God be using this season to prepare me?

Write honestly. This is between you and God.

Inner Goal / Mindset Shift

Today, I honor what God has placed in my hands.
I trust that faithfulness in small things matters.

5. What You Carry Still Matters

Scripture
"What do you have in your hand?"
— Exodus 4:2

Biblical Reflection

Moses focused on what he lacked, but God focused on what he already carried. A simple staff became the instrument God used to perform miracles. What Moses dismissed, God chose to use.

God does not wait for us to acquire more before He moves. He begins with what we already hold.

Invitation to Stillness

Sit quietly and breathe.
Ask God to reveal what you already have.
Notice any resistance or surprise.

Writing Prompt

Set a timer for **10 minutes**.

What skills, experiences, or wisdom do I already carry?

Where have I assumed it wasn't enough?

Write honestly. This is between you and God.

Inner Goal / Mindset Shift

Today, I stop overlooking what God has already given me.
I trust that what I carry still has purpose.

6. You Are Not Behind — You Are Becoming

Scripture
"Being confident of this, that He who began a good work in you will carry it on to completion."
— Philippians 1:6

Biblical Reflection

Growth does not happen on a straight timeline. Joseph's journey included delay, betrayal, and waiting. Yet none of it stopped what God was forming in him. Becoming takes time.

God does not rush formation. What feels slow may be necessary.

Invitation to Stillness

Breathe deeply.
Release urgency.
Allow God's timing to feel safe.

Writing Prompt

Set a timer for **10 minutes**.

Where have I been telling myself I'm behind?

What evidence exists that God is still working in me?

Write honestly. This is between you and God.

Inner Goal / Mindset Shift

Today, I release comparison.
I trust the pace of my becoming.

7. This Is Not Where Your Story Ends

Scripture
"Weeping may endure for a night, but joy comes in the morning."
— Psalm 30:5

Biblical Reflection

Many in Scripture experienced endings that felt final — loss, exile, grief. Yet God repeatedly proved that what looks like an ending is often a transition. God is not limited by chapters we don't understand.

Your current season does not define your final outcome.

Invitation to Stillness

Sit with this truth.
Breathe slowly.
Allow hope to exist without forcing it.

Writing Prompt

Set a timer for **10 minutes**.

What part of my life feels finished or hopeless right now?

What would it mean to trust that God is not done yet?

Write honestly. This is between you and God.

Inner Goal / Mindset Shift

Today, I allow hope to remain present.
I trust that God is still writing my story.

8. Faith Does Not Expire

Scripture
"Jesus Christ is the same yesterday and today and forever."
— Hebrews 13:8

Biblical Reflection

Faith is not something we age out of. Anna and Simeon waited decades to see God's promise fulfilled. Their faith remained alive because they stayed present and expectant.

Faith matures with time. It does not weaken unless we abandon it.

Invitation to Stillness

Pause.
Breathe.
Remember what God has already done.

Writing Prompt

Set a timer for **10 minutes**.

Where has my faith grown quieter over time?

What would it look like to engage God daily again?

Write honestly. This is between you and God.

Inner Goal / Mindset Shift

Today, I recommit to daily faith.
I trust that God is still present and active in my life.

9. Stop Making Peace with Less

Scripture
"Now to Him who is able to do immeasurably more than all we ask or imagine."
— Ephesians 3:20

Biblical Reflection

God never asked His people to settle — He asked them to trust. Yet over time, many lowered their expectations to protect themselves from disappointment. God's promises were not reduced, but people's belief in what was possible quietly was.

God does not call us to force outcomes, but He does call us to stop agreeing with limitation. Peace that comes from giving up is not the same as peace that comes from faith.

Invitation to Stillness

Sit quietly with this scripture.
Breathe deeply.
Notice where you have adjusted your expectations to avoid pain.

Writing Prompt

Set a timer for **10 minutes**.

Where have I made peace with less than what I once hoped for?

What might God be inviting me to believe again?

Write honestly. This is between you and God.

Inner Goal / Mindset Shift

Today, I release agreement with limitation.
I remain open to what God can still do.

10. God Can Still Use What Feels Unfinished

Scripture
"Being confident of this, that He who began a good work in you will carry it on to completion."
— Philippians 1:6

Biblical Reflection

Many people in Scripture were called before they felt complete. God does not wait for perfection before He works. What feels unfinished to you may still be forming under His care.

God's work is not rushed, but it is intentional. What He begins, He continues.

Invitation to Stillness

Pause.
Breathe slowly.
Allow yourself to feel unfinished without judgment.

Writing Prompt

Set a timer for **10 minutes**.

What part of my life feels incomplete or unresolved?

How might God still be working in this area?

Write honestly. This is between you and God.

Inner Goal / Mindset Shift

Today, I stop shaming what is still forming.
I trust God's process in my life.

11. You Were Not Forgotten

Scripture
"Can a mother forget the baby at her breast? Though she may forget, I will not forget you."
— Isaiah 49:15

Biblical Reflection

There were moments when God's people felt overlooked and unseen. Yet God spoke clearly — reminding them that His attention never wavered. Delay does not mean abandonment.

Even in quiet seasons, God remains present and attentive.

Invitation to Stillness

Sit with this truth.
Breathe deeply.
Let reassurance replace fear.

Writing Prompt

Set a timer for **10 minutes**.

Where have I felt unseen or overlooked?

What would it mean to believe God still sees me fully?

Write honestly. This is between you and God.

Inner Goal / Mindset Shift

Today, I reject the belief that I've been forgotten.
I trust that God remains attentive to my life.

12. Your Voice Was Never Meant to Disappear

Scripture
"I have put my words in your mouth."
— Isaiah 51:16

Biblical Reflection

God repeatedly chose people who doubted their ability to speak. Moses, Jeremiah, and Esther all hesitated. Yet God reminded them that He provides the words when the moment comes.

Silence may feel safer, but obedience often requires expression.

Invitation to Stillness

Pause.
Breathe.
Ask God where He is inviting you to speak again.

Writing Prompt

Set a timer for **10 minutes**.

Where have I grown quieter than God intended?

What truth have I been holding back?

Write honestly. This is between you and God.

Inner Goal / Mindset Shift

Today, I honor my voice.
I trust God to guide my words.

13. Waiting Is Not Wasted

Scripture
"But those who wait on the Lord shall renew their strength."
— Isaiah 40:31

Biblical Reflection

Waiting often feels like stagnation, but Scripture shows it as preparation. Joseph waited years before seeing fulfillment, yet nothing was lost. God was shaping endurance, wisdom, and humility.

Waiting strengthens what rushing would weaken.

Invitation to Stillness

Sit quietly.
Breathe slowly.
Release urgency.

Writing Prompt

Set a timer for **10 minutes**.

What am I currently waiting for?

How might God be using this waiting season?

Write honestly. This is between you and God.

Inner Goal / Mindset Shift

Today, I trust the purpose of waiting.
I allow God to renew my strength.

14. You Are Allowed to Want More

Scripture
"Delight yourself in the Lord, and He will give you the desires of your heart."
— Psalm 37:4

Biblical Reflection

Desire is not the enemy of faith. God places longings within us to draw us closer to Him. When aligned with God, desire becomes direction — not distraction.

Wanting more does not mean you are ungrateful. It may mean you are listening.

Invitation to Stillness

Pause and breathe.
Let desire surface without judgment.
Invite God into it.

Writing Prompt

Set a timer for **10 minutes**.

What desire have I been suppressing or dismissing?

How might this desire align with God's purpose for me?

Write honestly. This is between you and God.

Inner Goal / Mindset Shift

Today, I allow myself to desire with God.
I trust Him to shape what I long for.

15. What God Planted in You Is Still Alive

Scripture
"He who calls you is faithful, and He will do it."
— 1 Thessalonians 5:24

Biblical Reflection

There were moments when Sarah believed her season had passed. Time had moved on, and hope felt unreasonable. Yet God had not forgotten what He promised. What appeared dormant was still alive under His care.

God's promises do not expire. What He planted in you may look quiet, but it is not dead.

Invitation to Stillness

Sit quietly with this scripture.
Breathe slowly.
Allow hope to exist again.

Writing Prompt

Set a timer for **10 minutes**.

What promise or dream feels dormant in my life?

What would it mean to believe God is still faithful to it?

Write honestly. This is between you and God.

Inner Goal / Mindset Shift

Today, I trust that what God planted in me is still alive.
I remain open to His faithfulness.

16. Do Not Despise Where You Are

Scripture
"The Lord directs the steps of the godly."
— Psalm 37:23

Biblical Reflection

Many people in Scripture did not recognize the importance of where they stood. Places that felt ordinary were often preparation grounds. God works just as intentionally in quiet seasons as He does in visible ones.

Where you are right now is not random.

Invitation to Stillness

Pause.
Breathe deeply.
Allow the present moment to feel intentional.

Writing Prompt

Set a timer for **10 minutes**.

Where am I currently resisting my present season?

How might God be working here, even if I don't see it yet?

Write honestly. This is between you and God.

Inner Goal / Mindset Shift

Today, I honor where God has placed me.
I trust His direction in this season.

17. You Are Not Too Old for New Obedience

Scripture
"So Samuel did what the Lord said."
— 1 Samuel 16:4

Biblical Reflection

Samuel was well into life when God asked him to anoint a new king. Obedience did not stop because time passed. God continued to give direction, and Samuel continued to listen.

Obedience is not limited by age — it is sustained by willingness.

Invitation to Stillness

Sit quietly.
Breathe.
Ask God what obedience looks like now.

Writing Prompt

Set a timer for **10 minutes**.

Where might God be inviting me to obey again?

What fear or hesitation comes up when I consider this?

Write honestly. This is between you and God.

Inner Goal / Mindset Shift

Today, I remain willing to obey God.
I trust His leading at every age.

18. God Works Through the Willing, Not the Ready

Scripture
"Here am I. Send me!"
— Isaiah 6:8

Biblical Reflection

Isaiah did not claim readiness — he offered availability. God did not ask for perfection, only willingness. Throughout Scripture, God moves through those who show up honestly.

Willing hearts make room for divine work.

Invitation to Stillness

Pause.
Breathe slowly.
Release the need to feel ready.

Writing Prompt

Set a timer for **10 minutes**.

Where have I been waiting to feel 'ready' before acting?

What would change if I offered willingness instead?

Write honestly. This is between you and God.

Inner Goal / Mindset Shift

Today, I offer willingness over readiness.
I trust God to equip me as I move.

19. You Don't Need Permission to Begin Again

Scripture
"Forget the former things; do not dwell on the past."
— Isaiah 43:18

Biblical Reflection

God consistently invited His people forward — even after mistakes, losses, and failures. New beginnings were offered without shame. God does not require approval from your past to move you forward.

Grace opens doors that regret tries to close.

Invitation to Stillness

Sit quietly.
Breathe deeply.
Release the weight of what has already passed.

Writing Prompt

Set a timer for **10 minutes**.

What am I ready to begin again?

What belief has been holding me back from starting?

Write honestly. This is between you and God.

Inner Goal / Mindset Shift

Today, I release the need for permission.
I accept God's invitation to begin again.

20. This Is a Season of Revelation

Scripture
"Call to me and I will answer you and tell you great and unsearchable things."
— Jeremiah 33:3

Biblical Reflection

Revelation often comes in quieter seasons, when distractions fall away. God reveals truth not to overwhelm, but to guide. Stillness creates space for clarity.

God speaks when we listen.

Invitation to Stillness

Pause.
Breathe slowly.
Invite God to reveal what you need to see.

Writing Prompt

Set a timer for **10 minutes**.

What truth feels ready to surface in my life?

How can I create more space to hear God clearly?

Write honestly. This is between you and God.

Inner Goal / Mindset Shift

Today, I remain open to God's revelation.
I trust Him to guide me with clarity.

21. Your Life Still Has Weight

Scripture
"You are God's workmanship, created in Christ Jesus to do good works, which God prepared in advance for us to do."
— Ephesians 2:10

Biblical Reflection

There were many moments in Scripture when God's people believed their lives no longer carried meaning. After exile, after loss, after failure, they questioned whether they still mattered. Yet God repeatedly reminded them that He does not create anything casually. Every life is shaped with intention, even when the person living it feels overlooked or ordinary.

God's workmanship is not defined by visibility or applause. It is defined by purpose. Even when your life feels quiet or repetitive, God still assigns weight to your obedience, your prayers, your presence, and your endurance. You are not a placeholder in someone else's story. You are part of God's design — right now, not someday later.

Invitation to Stillness

Sit quietly.
Breathe deeply.
Let yourself matter again.

Writing Prompt

Set a timer for **10 minutes**.

Where have I been treating my life as insignificant or replaceable?

What changes when I remember I was created with intention?

Write honestly. This is between you and God.

Inner Goal / Mindset Shift

Today, I honor the weight of my life.
I accept that God created me with purpose.

Scriptures for the Week

- **Feeling insignificant?** Read *Psalm 139:13–14*

- **Feeling overlooked?** Study *Isaiah 43:1*

- **Feeling unsure of purpose?** Meditate on *Romans 8:28*

22. Silence Is Not the Same as Peace

Scripture
"Pour out your hearts to Him, for God is our refuge."
— Psalm 62:8

Biblical Reflection

Many people grow quiet not because they are at peace, but because they are tired. Scripture shows us that God never asked His people to disappear emotionally. He invited them to bring everything — grief, confusion, anger, fear — directly to Him. Silence can be a form of protection, but it can also become a place where pain hides and grows.

Peace is not the absence of emotion; it is the presence of God within it. When we stop expressing what is happening inside us, we don't become stronger — we become numb. God offers refuge, not suppression. He can only heal what we are willing to bring into the light.

Invitation to Stillness

Pause.
Breathe slowly.
Notice the difference between calm and numbness.

Writing Prompt

Set a timer for **10 minutes**.

Where have I chosen silence instead of honesty?

What emotion might God be inviting me to express?

Write honestly. This is between you and God.

Inner Goal / Mindset Shift

Today, I allow myself to be honest with God.
I trust Him with my emotions.

Scriptures for the Week

- **Feeling overwhelmed?** Read *Matthew 11:28–30*
- **Feeling emotionally shut down?** Study *Psalm 34:18*
- **Feeling afraid to open up?** Meditate on *1 Peter 5:7*

23. God Does Not Rush Purpose

Scripture
"At the proper time we will reap a harvest if we do not give up."
— Galatians 6:9

Biblical Reflection

God has never been hurried by human timelines. Throughout Scripture, purpose unfolds slowly so it can last. Abraham waited decades. Joseph endured years of delay. Moses lived an entire lifetime before stepping fully into his calling. God is not late — He is intentional.

Rushing what God is growing can weaken what He intends to sustain. Delay is not denial; it is often protection. Purpose matures in patience, and strength develops in waiting. God knows exactly when you will be ready for what He has promised.

Invitation to Stillness

Sit quietly.
Breathe deeply.
Release urgency.

Writing Prompt

Set a timer for **10 minutes**.

Where have I been rushing God's timing?

What might patience be producing in me?

Write honestly. This is between you and God.

Inner Goal / Mindset Shift

Today, I trust God's timing.
I allow purpose to unfold naturally.

Scriptures for the Week

- **Feeling impatient?** Read *Psalm 27:14*
- **Feeling discouraged by delay?** Study *Habakkuk 2:3*
- **Feeling tired of waiting?** Meditate on *Isaiah 40:31*

24. You Are Stronger Than You Think

Scripture
"My grace is sufficient for you, for My power is made perfect in weakness."
— 2 Corinthians 12:9

Biblical Reflection

God's strength often appears where people feel weakest. Scripture consistently shows that weakness does not disqualify — it creates space for God's power. Paul learned that his limitations were not something to hide, but something God could work through.

The fact that you are still here is evidence of strength you may not recognize yet. Grace has carried you through moments you thought would break you. Strength is not always loud or visible — sometimes it looks like endurance.

Invitation to Stillness

Pause.
Breathe slowly.
Acknowledge what you've endured.

Writing Prompt

Set a timer for **10 minutes**.

What challenges have I already survived?

How has God sustained me through them?

Write honestly. This is between you and God.

Inner Goal / Mindset Shift

Today, I acknowledge my strength.
I trust God's grace working through me.

Scriptures for the Week

- **Feeling weak?** Read *Isaiah 41:10*
- **Feeling worn down?** Study *Psalm 46:1*
- **Feeling like giving up?** Meditate on *2 Corinthians 4:16*

25. Your Yes Still Carries Power

Scripture
"Behold, I am the servant of the Lord; let it be to me according to your word."
— Luke 1:38

Biblical Reflection

Mary's yes was quiet, private, and costly — yet it changed history. God continues to move through willing hearts, not perfect ones. Obedience does not lose its power with age, experience, or past mistakes.

Your yes still matters because God is still moving. One obedient response can open doors you never expected. God honors willingness.

Invitation to Stillness

Sit quietly.
Breathe deeply.
Consider where God may be inviting your yes.

Writing Prompt

Set a timer for **10 minutes**.

Where might God be asking for my yes?

What fear or hope comes up when I consider it?

Write honestly. This is between you and God.

Inner Goal / Mindset Shift

Today, I remain open to obedience.
I trust that my yes still carries power.

Scriptures for the Week

- **Feeling afraid to say yes?** Read *Joshua 1:9*
- **Feeling uncertain?** Study *Proverbs 3:5–6*
- **Feeling hesitant?** Meditate on *Romans 12:1*

26. Faith Grows in Small, Daily Choices

Scripture
"Whoever can be trusted with very little can also be trusted with much."
— Luke 16:10

Biblical Reflection

Faith is not built in moments of intensity alone — it is formed through consistency. Scripture shows that God honors small, repeated acts of trust. Daily obedience shapes deep roots. Faith that lasts is practiced quietly.

God does not ask for perfection, only presence. What you choose daily matters more than what you promise occasionally.

Invitation to Stillness

Pause.
Breathe.
Focus on today.

Writing Prompt

Set a timer for **10 minutes**.

What small daily choice could strengthen my faith?

How can I show up consistently rather than perfectly?

Write honestly. This is between you and God.

Inner Goal / Mindset Shift

Today, I choose faith in small ways.
I trust God with daily obedience.

Scriptures for the Week

- **Feeling inconsistent?** Read *Lamentations 3:22–23*
- **Feeling distracted?** Study *Matthew 6:33*
- **Feeling spiritually dry?** Meditate on *John 15:4*

27. You Are Not Meant to Live Numb

Scripture

"I have come that they may have life, and have it to the full."
— John 10:10

Biblical Reflection

God never intended for life with Him to feel dull, flat, or emotionally shut down. Throughout Scripture, God's people felt deeply — joy, sorrow, anger, awe — and God met them in all of it. Numbness is often a response to pain we didn't know how to process, not a sign of strength or maturity.

Jesus came to restore fullness, not just survival. Feeling again can be uncomfortable, but it is also where healing begins. God does not ask you to turn your heart off to stay safe — He invites you to bring it back to life in His presence.

Invitation to Stillness

Sit quietly.
Breathe slowly.
Notice where you've gone numb to cope.

Writing Prompt

Set a timer for **10 minutes**.

Where in my life do I feel emotionally disconnected or shut down?

What emotion might God be inviting me to feel and process safely?

Write honestly. This is between you and God.

Inner Goal / Mindset Shift

Today, I allow myself to feel again.
I trust God to meet me in my emotions.

Scriptures for the Week

- **Feeling numb?** Read *Psalm 147:3*

- **Feeling overwhelmed by emotion?** Study *Psalm 42:11*

- **Feeling disconnected from joy?** Meditate on *Nehemiah 8:10*

28. God Can Work With What You Have

Scripture
"What do you have in your house?"
— 2 Kings 4:2

Biblical Reflection

When the widow felt desperate and lacking, God did not ask her for what she didn't have. He asked her to notice what was already in her house. What seemed small and insufficient became the very thing God multiplied.

God often begins with what we overlook. He does not wait for abundance before He acts — He creates abundance through obedience. What you already have may be more than you realize.

Invitation to Stillness

Pause.
Breathe deeply.
Ask God to show you what you already hold.

Writing Prompt

Set a timer for **10 minutes**.

What resources, skills, or support do I already have?

Where have I been focusing on lack instead of provision?

Write honestly. This is between you and God.

Inner Goal / Mindset Shift

Today, I acknowledge what I already have.
I trust God to work through it.

Scriptures for the Week

- **Feeling inadequate?** Read *Exodus 4:2*
- **Feeling financially anxious?** Study *Philippians 4:19*
- **Feeling unsure of next steps?** Meditate on *Proverbs 16:9*

29. You Are Still Becoming Who God Spoke

Scripture
"Let us not become weary in doing good."
— Galatians 6:9

Biblical Reflection

God speaks identity before we see the evidence. David was anointed king long before he sat on the throne. Becoming takes time, pressure, and patience. Weariness does not mean you are failing — it means you are still in the process.

God's word over your life does not expire because it hasn't fully appeared yet. You are still becoming.

Invitation to Stillness

Sit quietly.
Breathe slowly.
Let yourself be in process.

Writing Prompt

Set a timer for **10 minutes**.

What identity or calling has God spoken over me that I'm still growing into?

Where do I feel tired in the becoming process?

Write honestly. This is between you and God.

Inner Goal / Mindset Shift

Today, I give myself grace to become.
I trust God's word over my life.

Scriptures for the Week

- **Feeling weary?** Read *Isaiah 40:29*
- **Feeling discouraged?** Study *Hebrews 12:11*
- **Feeling uncertain about identity?** Meditate on *Romans 8:1*

30. Your Past Does Not Disqualify You

Scripture
"Therefore, if anyone is in Christ, the new creation has come."
— 2 Corinthians 5:17

Biblical Reflection

Scripture is filled with people who carried complicated pasts — yet God did not define them by their worst moments. Paul persecuted believers. Peter denied Jesus. Rahab carried a reputation she couldn't erase. God still used them powerfully.

Your past may shape you, but it does not own you. God redeems what once felt disqualifying and uses it for His glory.

Invitation to Stillness

Pause.
Breathe deeply.
Release shame.

What would returning look like gently, not dramatically?

Write honestly. This is between you and God.

Inner Goal / Mindset Shift

Today, I respond to God's invitation to return.
I move back toward myself and Him.

32. God Is Still Writing Your Story

Scripture
"I know the plans I have for you."
— Jeremiah 29:11

Biblical Reflection

God's plans do not stop mid-story. Even when chapters feel unclear or slow, He continues writing. Scripture reminds us that God sees beyond the page we're currently on.

Your story is not stalled — it is unfolding.

Invitation to Stillness

Pause.
Breathe deeply.
Trust the Author.

Writing Prompt

Set a timer for **10 minutes**.

What chapter of my life am I currently in?

What would it mean to trust God with what comes next?

Write honestly. This is between you and God.

Inner Goal / Mindset Shift

Today, I trust God with my story.
I remain open to what He is still writing.

33. You Were Never Meant to Go Quiet

Scripture
"Let your light shine before others."
— Matthew 5:16

Biblical Reflection

Throughout Scripture, God continually called His people out of hiding. Esther was told she could not remain silent. Jeremiah was reminded that God's words were placed in his mouth. Silence may feel safer, but obedience often requires visibility. God does not call us to disappear when life becomes heavy — He calls us to remain present.

Going quiet is rarely about humility; it is often about fear, exhaustion, or disappointment. But God's light in you was never meant to dim with time. The same God who called you before is still calling you now. Your voice, your presence, and your obedience still matter.

Invitation to Stillness

Sit quietly.
Breathe deeply.
Ask God where He is inviting you to show up again.

Writing Prompt

Set a timer for **10 minutes**.

Where have I been hiding or shrinking myself?

What would it look like to stay visible with God's help?

Write honestly. This is between you and God.

Inner Goal / Mindset Shift

Today, I choose presence over hiding.
I allow God's light to move through me again.

Scriptures for the Week

- **Feeling afraid to be seen?** Read *Esther 4:14*
- **Feeling unsure of your voice?** Study *Jeremiah 1:9*
- **Feeling called but hesitant?** Meditate on *Matthew 5:14–16*

34. Stay Present — God Is Here

Scripture
"Surely I am with you always."
— Matthew 28:20

Biblical Reflection

God's presence is not reserved for mountaintop moments. He promises to be with us in ordinary days, unanswered questions, and quiet routines. Scripture reminds us that God does not abandon us in the middle of the journey — He walks with us through it.

Presence changes everything. When we stay present, fear loses its grip and faith has room to breathe. God is not waiting for you to arrive somewhere else. He is already here.

Invitation to Stillness

Pause.
Breathe slowly.
Let God's nearness feel real.

Writing Prompt

Set a timer for **10 minutes**.

Where have I been mentally or emotionally absent from my life?

What would it look like to stay present with God today?

Write honestly. This is between you and God.

Inner Goal / Mindset Shift

Today, I choose presence over distraction.
I trust that God is with me here.

Scriptures for the Week

- **Feeling anxious?** Read *Psalm 46:10*

- **Feeling overwhelmed?** Study *Deuteronomy 31:6*

- **Feeling alone?** Meditate on *Isaiah 41:13*

35. Begin Again, With God

Scripture
"Because of the Lord's great love we are not consumed; His mercies are new every morning."
— Lamentations 3:22–23

Biblical Reflection

Scripture shows us that God specializes in beginnings. New mornings. New mercies. New paths forward. Beginning again is not failure — it is faith in motion. God does not shame us for needing renewal. He provides it.

No matter what age you are, no matter how many times you've started over, God's invitation remains open. You are allowed to begin again — with Him. This is not the end of your story. It is a continuation, guided by grace.

Invitation to Stillness

Sit quietly.
Breathe deeply.
Receive the permission to begin again.

Writing Prompt

Set a timer for **10 minutes**.

What does beginning again mean for me right now?

What am I ready to place in God's hands moving forward?

Write honestly. This is between you and God.

Inner Goal / Mindset Shift

Today, I accept God's invitation to begin again.
I move forward with grace, trust, and faith.

Scriptures for the Week

- **Feeling weary?** Read *Isaiah 43:19*

- **Feeling uncertain about the future?** Study *Proverbs 16:3*

- **Feeling hopeful but cautious?** Meditate on *Philippians 1:6*

A Final Study: Drawing Closer to God

Before you begin, pause.
Take one slow breath.
Invite God into this moment.

For each question, choose **A, B, or C** — not because one is better, but because **each answer reveals a different way God is meeting you**.

All answers are true.
All answers are holy.

1. When I think about my age right now, I feel God inviting me to:

A. Trust Him more deeply than I ever have before
B. Release old timelines and rest in His timing
C. Step forward with the wisdom I've gained

2. As I studied these scriptures, I noticed God speaking to me through:

A. Quiet reassurance
B. Gentle conviction
C. Renewed hope

3. When I sit with God in stillness, I am learning to:

A. Listen instead of rush
B. Be honest instead of strong
C. Rest instead of strive

4. In this season of my life, God is teaching me that growth looks like:

A. Faithfulness in small moments
B. Patience with the process
C. Trust in what I cannot yet see

5. When I reflect on my past, I now see God as someone who was:

A. Present, even when I didn't notice
B. Protective, even when I felt delayed
C. Faithful, even when I doubted

6. As I move forward from this book, I feel God calling me to:

A. Pray more honestly
B. Live more intentionally
C. Walk more closely with Him

7. When fear or doubt tries to return, I am reminded that God is:

A. With me
B. For me
C. Working through me

8. In this next chapter of my life, I believe God wants me to focus on:

A. Presence
B. Obedience
C. Trust

9. As I think about beginning again, I now understand that God's mercy is:

A. New every morning
B. Not limited by age
C. Greater than my mistakes

10. Right now, my relationship with God feels like an invitation to:

A. Go deeper
B. Stay open
C. Keep walking

How to Receive This Study

There is no score to calculate.
Instead, look back at the letters you chose most often.

- If **A** stood out, God may be inviting you into **deeper trust and honesty**.

- If **B** stood out, God may be inviting you into **rest and surrender**.

- If **C** stood out, God may be inviting you into **faithful movement and confidence**.

All three are signs of closeness.
All three are ways God draws His people near.

A Closing Truth

No matter your age,
no matter your pace,
no matter how many times you've begun again —

God is not finished with you.

35 is not old.
It is aware.
It is grounded.
It is ready.

And you are closer to God now than you were before you turned this page.

About the Author

Ebony Greenfield is a writer, creative, and faith-centered storyteller with a **Master's degree in Communication**. Her work lives at the intersection of reflection, faith, creativity, and personal growth. She is passionate about helping people reconnect with their inner world, their voice, and their relationship with God through honest self-exploration and spiritual grounding.

In addition to writing, Ebony creates music under the name **ImJarra**, blending emotion, storytelling, and innovation. Her music—both traditional and AI-assisted—is available to stream on all major platforms. Through sound and reflection, she explores themes of identity, healing, and becoming.

You can connect with Ebony and explore more of her work here:

- **Instagram:** @ImJarra
- **Facebook:** ImJarra
- **YouTube:** ImJarra

Hi — I hope you enjoyed the read today. Thank you for spending time with these pages and for choosing to show up for yourself and for God. May you continue growing, listening, and becoming long after you close this book

Made in the USA
Coppell, TX
14 January 2026